DELILAH'S
LAP

DELILAH'S
LAP

TERRANCE D BAKER

XULON ELITE

Xulon Press Elite
2301 Lucien Way #415
Maitland, FL 32751
407.339.4217
www.xulonpress.com

Paperback ISBN-13: 978-1-66283-717-3
Ebook ISBN-13: 978-1-66283-718-0

Table of Contents

Introduction vii

Chapter 1: The Three Egos 1

Chapter 2: The Power of a Woman 9

Chapter 3: The Party Crashers 15

Chapter 4: The Necessity of Delilah. .19

Chapter 5: The Desired Effect. 31

Chapter 6: The Training Process. 37

Chapter 7: By Any Other Name 43

Chapter 8: Basic Instinct 49

Chapter 9: The Skilled Fisherman 57

Chapter 10: The Breadcrumb Trail. 63

Book Summary. 69

About the Author 71

Dedication. 73

Introduction

Very few of us can say we have never had an experience in Delilah's Lap. The experience of having our lust and desire completely uncaged and wreaking havoc in our lives. The experience of putting ourselves in a position that only God can get us out of. The experience of thinking we have everything we want only to find out we have nothing. Some of us escape because we heed the warnings, some of us get away by the skin of our teeth, but some of us are not fortunate enough to escape the clutches and consequences of Delilah's Lap. We get trapped by our own desire of what we think we want, often neglecting the fact that the things we are chasing sometimes are already in our possession. That's the smoke and mirror trick the enemy uses against us, luring us to try to gain what we already have. The great philosopher Socrates, who some refer to as the "Father of Western Philosophy," said, "He who is not contented with what he has would not be contented with what he would like to have." The philosopher's wisdom was speaking to those of us seduced by the allure of greed. For instance, the rich man, who already has more than enough money, becomes obsessed with gaining more. The overeater who has already filled his stomach but continues to eat. These are just a couple of examples of greed that is fueled by lust and desire, which by the way is the area of expertise for Delilah. She quickly seizes that area of fragility and impregnates that inability to be satisfied. That inability is the very nature of lust and desire. Lust and desire are feelings we all go through at some point in our lives. We may pull from different branches, but we all have bitten fruit from the poisonous tree. Most of us very seldom put any thought into where and what those feelings may lead us to. Often, there are dangerous conclusions that arise when we capitulate to these passions. The consequences in the average case are the last thing we think of during the culmination of these relationships, but we quickly find ourselves in a position of contrition when and if worse comes to worst. Both lust and desire are natural, and because they are natural, they are also what many of us use to legitimize our actions if we choose to relinquish our authority to these sensations. Some of us have even convinced ourselves and others that the surrender to these actions was uncontrollable. This is far from the truth because both lust and desire are completely under our own dictation. We all make a conscious decision to surrender or not to the will of these feelings. Though there are times when fighting to acquiesce to these feelings is more difficult than other times, but this does not change the fact that the authority is still within our hands. Let's use, for example, something that many Christians struggle with—fasting. During a water fast, the urge to eat is great because we have deprived ourselves of something our body wants and usually gets. We have trained our minds and bodies to surrender to food even though in many cases we don't even really want it. Especially here in America, most of us don't really experience the actual definition of hunger; we usually experience habit. Food is so easily accessible that we have completely confused our want of it with our need for it. Food is a necessity for the sustaining of life, but when there is an overabundance of it, we sometimes confuse want and need. Therefore, many of us same Christians who have no trouble deciding who is going to hell, what sin is an abomination to God, and who needs to be put out of the church have such a hard time giving up food for even a short period of time, even though Jesus said, **"16. Moreover, when ye fast, be not, as the hypocrites..." (Matthew 6:16 KJV)**. He didn't say, if you fast, or if you want to fast, he said WHEN you fast. Suddenly even the most finger-pointing saints are faced with the most arduous of demands. Most of us don't even realize the most basic principle of fasting or the greatness of its benefits. No matter how axiomatic it is, we normally omit the simplest truth. The truth is simply this: no matter how hard it is or how strong the impulse, no food gets in our mouth until we put it in there. I do realize that sounds like common sense, but how many of us use that common sense during this time of denial? Think of it. On a water fast, a large part of being successful is to not eat. Now this logic probably seems more onerous while you are fasting than when you are not. Still, the simple fact is if you don't put food in your mouth, it doesn't get in. My point is simply this: though we seldom use our best judgment about it, lust, like fasting, is under the jurisdiction of us. Of course, there are other desires that I would assume require even more strength than fasting, but I dare not even attempt to cross into the lanes of anything I have not experienced or struggled with, such as drug addiction or alcoholism. I will only speak on the struggles I have encountered, and these encounters I experienced were controllable, so to me making the claims that a controllable action is uncontrollable or even a mistake would be like the person who drinks and drives. In other words, no matter how you try to shape it—I lost my job, my spouse left me, I was depressed—none of it matters. It still was your fault because you made a choice to drink and drive. I will not deny, though, that the struggle with lust and desire is real, but nevertheless it is still a choice.

Mythological tales speak of a beautiful creature that was half woman and half fish. Some stories referred to her as a Siren and others as a Mermaid. The tale goes on to say she would lure sailors in with her beauty and the sound of her voice. This would mesmerize the sailors and they would be helpless to her spell, but this spell would ultimately lead to their death. Though this creature is only a myth, it does offer some form of explanation and example as to the power concupiscence has over the human mind and body.

Unlike the myth that insinuates the victim has no choice in the matter, realism begs to differ. Men and women alike have surrendered to the lecherous appetite of lust and desire. It is a powerful force that few seem to be able to find the will to counter. Some would call this a demonic stronghold that has plagued just as many women as it has men, but I will refer to this momentary gratification with long-term consequences in this writing as the spirit of Delilah. I will take a quick peek into who Delilah was and her nefarious accomplishments. Delilah the woman died thousands of years ago, but her spirit lives on. Even today that spirit is still inveigling many to lay their head in Delilah's Lap.

Chapter 1

The Three Egos

18. When Delilah realized that he had told her his secret, she sent for the Philistine tyrants, telling them, "Come quickly—this time he's told me the truth." They came, bringing the bribe money. 19. When she got him to sleep, his head on her lap, she motioned to a man to cut off the seven braids of his hair. Immediately he began to grow weak. His strength drained from him. 20. Then she said, "The Philistines are on you, Samson!" He woke up, thinking, "I'll go out, like always, and shake free." He didn't realize that God had abandoned him. 21. The Philistines grabbed him, gouged out his eyes, and took him down to Gaza. They shackled him in irons and put him to the work of grinding in the prison (Judges 16:18–21 MSG).

The story of Samson and Delilah is a story that has been told in churches and bible studies all over the world. It's a story of passion, lies, deceit, and death. How could any of us forget the story of the strongest man the world has ever known who was defeated by the woman whose lap he laid his head in. In the biblical illustration Delilah is described as female, but the spirit of Delilah is genderless. Delilah can be male or female. This spirit can be feminine or masculine. It is an extremely promiscuous spirit. It uses its sexual allure as a method of control for personal gain as well as destruction. Delilah takes on whatever form that is needed to blind and separate her prey from their source. If love is needed, this spirit presents the illusion of love; if sex is needed, it happily offers sex. This spirit is willing to give whatever it takes to lower the guard of her mark. The spirit of Delilah is a spirit of duplicity. It's a spirit that mainly uses its physical attributes of attraction and intimacy to bring down its intended target, or from a biblical reference to cut Samson's hair. It attacks in the most vulnerable of places, and most of the time, especially in men, that place is the ego. The bigger your ego, the more vulnerable you are. Delilah can sense the ego and vulnerability in a man like a shark that smells blood in the water. The spirit of Delilah is well versed and skilled in lying and knows how to feed the ego. In my experience and belief an ego, especially the ego of a man, comes in three forms. The overfed, the underfed, and the want to be fed. Whichever she finds within her mark is where she will concentrate her focus. If her target steps into the figurative boxing ring with his ribs bandaged up, she shows no mercy. The ribs become her point of attack, for that is the most axiomatic area of debility. She is going to focus all her efforts on the bandaged ribs. Once Delilah begins to feed one of the three egos, and in some cases all three, and she sees that her target is accepting the nutrients she is offering, she will continue to feed and overfeed her prey. She'll tell him what he needs to hear. For her there is no consciousness of the lies she is willing to tell. Even if the lie is unbelievable, she knows to hold fast to that lie until there is absolute proof that her words are not true. She will ride her lie until the wheels fall off, but when they do, she'll buy another set. Delilah is extremely skilled in knowing which lie to tell each ego. For instance, if the target has an overfed ego, she will continue to overfeed what he wants to believe. She becomes a nefarious nurse who is caring for a diabetic patient. See, to a diabetic, food can be your best friend and your worst enemy all at the same time. There are times that a diabetic must have food because their levels are too low, but there are also times that the same foods that brought those levels to a place of normality can kill them. Much like the nefarious nurse, Delilah knows this, so the overfed ego is her easiest target.

The overfed ego is one who doesn't need the reassurance of confidence, he doesn't need to be told because he already believes, so he is an easy target for her because in him the snowball is already rolling downhill, and Delilah needs little to no effort to continue this motion. It's not difficult to convince the overfed ego of what he already believes. If he believes he is handsome, she will tell him how much more handsome he is. "You are the sexiest and most handsome man I have ever been with." Even his flaws she will capitalize on. If one of his flaws is his stomach, she will convince him that this is one of the things that most attracted her to him. She will make him believe that even his flaw is a strength. She'll give him what he desires to have and sometimes even what he may need, but she does it in excess. Though there is nothing wrong with having self-confidence, for this can be beneficial, overconfidence in many cases can give birth to an uncontrollable monster. So, Delilah helps to encourage the blur in the line between confidence and overconfidence. Delilah will seduce the overfed with his own thoughts of himself. His egotistical personality is his Achilles' heel. She will make him believe he is the only man capable of causing her to love. She will make him feel like and even refer to him as her king. She will sometimes even offer the appearance of submission to him and make him believe he is the only man she has gone this far with. She creates the illusion of being the untamable stallion in the western movie that only the hero has the right stuff to tame. No matter how many other men she has been with, she will convince the overfed ego that he is the best she has ever experienced. "No one has ever made me feel or has ever done to me the things you do." These are magical words to the overfed because the overfed seeks to be known, seen, and remembered as the best.

One of the defenses, though seldom used, of the overfed is his ability to see who Delilah really is. Believe it or not, the overfed ego can see through all her lies and tricks. Many overfed egos recognize a cunning and deceitful behavior because they themselves are often just as cunning and deceitful as well. Yet the overfed ego usually has the proclivity of arrogance. This arrogance causes him to believe that even though he can see through Delilah's lies and her deception, he is the exception to the rule, and it won't happen to him. No matter what she does or how much she lies, that arrogance still makes him feel he is safe in her lap. He usually assumes it will or has happened to other men, but it won't happen to him. The overfed ego is like the old man from a story I heard some time ago.

Once upon a time there was an old farmer who was out looking over his land. He came across a snake that was dying. The old farmer had mercy on the snake, picked it up, took it home, and nursed it back to health. The farmer checked on the snake daily, to be reassured of the snake's progress. One morning the farmer came to check on the well-being of the snake. The farmer heard the rattling of the snake's tail but ignored the warnings. When the farmer was close enough, the snake bit the farmer. The farmer, being confused, asked the snake, "Why did you bite me? I brought you in and nursed you back to health when you were dying." The snake looked at the farmer with no remorse and said, "You knew I was a snake when you picked me up."

You see, the farmer had gained the proclivity of arrogance because up until that point the snake had never bit him. The farmer felt safe with someone he should not have felt safe around. This is much like the thought of the overfed ego. Because it has never happened to him before, he assumes it won't happen now. But often, if not most of the time, where there is no consequence of action, there is no lesson learned.

Next up is the underfed ego. This is the ego that must be built up. He is an easy target because he falls for anything Delilah says or does and won't fight back. It's not that the underfed can't fight, but he is just so afraid of losing Delilah that he accepts the abuse. Delilah runs over the top of him. He doesn't consider himself to be very attractive, so he allows Delilah to do anything she wants just so she will stay with him. If she says, "Sit," he sits. If she says, "Come," he comes. He has a very nonaggressive personality and he easily falls in love. Delilah will take advantage of him and won't even lie about it. Unlike the overfed who is a natural fighter, the underfed has no fight in him when it comes to Delilah. The overfed will fight back, but his arrogance usually causes him to be victimized. The underfed won't fight at all. He only wants a happy and peaceful life with Delilah. His personality is no match for her; she rules him with an iron hand and if it keeps her happy, he doesn't care. She makes ridiculous demands of him, and he agrees. He will give her what she wants, take her where she wants to go, and do what she wants him to do. The reason she will not even bother to lie to the underfed is because she knows his greatest fear is living without her. For the overfed, Delilah must lie with guileful strategy to keep any form of control. With the underfed she works by the power of the trepidation, which is enough to keep him under her dominance. The underfed is more like the donkey or the mule, a beast of burden that simply obeys, whereas the overfed is more like a bucking stallion horse that must be tamed. Many underfed egos will go so far as to marry Delilah, hoping the marriage will be the security he needs to hold her. In the movie *Coming to America*, the underfed would-be Imani Izzi, who followed the "whatever you like" approach, anything to keep her king, or in this case his queen, happy. The underfed is usually a nice guy who at the very least feels he doesn't have many options when it comes to women. He often settles for whatever he can get. So, when he gets an opportunity to have a Delilah in his life, she becomes like a dream come true and there is nothing he won't do to stay within the confines of that fantasy.

Then there is the want to be fed ego. We all know him as the one who wants to fit in with the cool kids. He will do anything he has to do to look like one of the crew. He was the one in school who would give away his lunch money if he could just hang with the "in crowd." To Delilah, he is an easy target because she makes him look like what he longs to look like. In some ways you could say the "want to be fed" ego uses Delilah just as much as she uses him. Her physical attributes give him status and position. To those within their proximity, she makes him look like he belongs. The mentality that is created is that if he can get a woman who looks like that, maybe there's more to him than previously assumed. The want to be fed really doesn't mind being used by Delilah because many times the illusion she creates for him is long-term. It's long-term because even after their relationship is over, he still gets to tell the stories of when he had Delilah. The want to be fed ego for Delilah is more like an ATM. For her he is an easy source of money, or a source to gain position. Now, that is not to say Delilah doesn't receive money and position from the other two egos, but the want to be fed is more of a business transaction. He is the cash cow. Within their relationship, because they both know their role, there is not a lot of confusion. He knows she wants his money, and she knows he wants her sex and the ability to use her name. So, he gives and so does she. Even though the want to be fed is not someone Delilah would normally choose, he serves a purpose. She finds solution to a problem in him.

Chapter 2

The Power of a Woman

To start things off, I think we really need to look at who Samson was to demonstrate the power Delilah had over him. Samson was born to be a fighter, sent by God to rescue the Israelites from the Philistines. The Bible says that Samson killed thousands of Philistine soldiers. Now, though Samson often beat them relatively easy, don't underestimate who the Philistine soldiers were. These were men trained in the art of war. These were brave men that were ready, willing, and able to kill at a moment's notice. Yet this one man that the Holy Spirit would come upon rendered all their skills, training, and power helpless and at his mercy. The Philistines plotted, planned, and schemed without any success to defeat Samson. How frustrating it must have been to have an enemy that you hate, yet all your efforts to defeat this enemy are thwarted. None of their strategists could devise a plan that could stop the great Samson. His strength was unmatched by any man, but what of a wo-man? Samson's biggest weakness was his inability to control his urges for the Philistine women. Time and time again, he would taunt his enemies with his presence, but like a fly too close to the spider web he eventually got caught. Ironically enough, Samson was repeatedly able to get away from the strength of the men but could not escape the power of a woman.

Physically the woman is often described as the weaker vessel. Yet down through history from the beginning of time up until this present day, the woman has demonstrated a power and ability that man after man has fallen prey and victim to. Adam walked with God in the Garden of Eden, yet he was powerless standing in front of Eve as she bit the fruit. David killed a giant with nothing more than a slingshot, yet he couldn't resist the power of Bathsheba as she bathed on the roof of her home. Samson was able to kill a lion with his bare hands after the Spirit of the Lord came upon him, but all his strength was no match for the power Delilah possessed. You see, we men are programmed to attack physically from the outside in, whereas the woman has learned to attack from the inside out. Often silent with the potential of being deadly, a woman can have the appearance of a gentle stream that glides over a rock creating sounds of beauty and at the same time have the destructive capability of a tsunami. Many times, her power is underestimated, which means she can be even more dangerous. Our most ferocious rival is not necessarily the one who is bigger, stronger, or even faster. Many times, our greatest opponent is the one we underestimate the most. Goliath saw no threat in David, so he underestimated him because of his size, never realizing that David held the giant's last breath inside of a small pouch. Samson saw no threat in Delilah so night after night he stuck his head inside the jaws of a hungry alligator.

Often the beauty of a woman is distracting to men. For this reason, we can safely conclude that the pulchritude of Delilah was stunning. I say her pulchritude was a safe conclusion because the Bible never definitively says that Samson and Delilah had sex. I believe it's a good assumption to think they did because he was a very sexually active man and, in many cases, sex is the avenue to the control of some men. Sometimes sex acts as a bit in the mouth of a horse. It communicates directional control from the rider. Men are not going to admit it, but when the rider says go left, we are going left. So, speaking from the position of a man, I can't think of too many other things Delilah could have offered Samson to make him give up his most valuable secret. The Bible does say she basically nagged Samson until he told her everything, but my assumption is that she nagged him before, during, or after sex.

The Bible seems to show Samson as a man with normal male attractions for the opposite sex. Like many of us, he does seem to have a thing for the forbidden. The Bible doesn't visit Samson's thoughts to question why there was such a desire for the Philistine women, but they must have possessed something, at least to him, that the Israelite women didn't have. This is no different from any other man. We all have our preferences. So, for that we cannot put Samson down. The Bible also lets us know he didn't have any problem paying a prostitute or a harlot, if you will, to enjoy a night with her. Maybe it was the thrill of the business transaction that appealed to him. The business transaction is a turn-on for some men because it gives a feeling of temporary ownership. Almost like the renting of a car, we know that at a certain time we must give it back but for that moment that car belongs to us. Therefore, we can do what we want to do with it. For that reason, oftentimes we do to the rental car things we would never do with our own car, get it? Or maybe for Samson, it was the fact that there were no games played with the prostitute. Some men get excited about this because of the prostitution contract. In the prostitution contract, there is no middleman. She doesn't offer dine-in services, only the drive-thru window. Drive up, pay for your food, and drive away. Possibly Samson was an adrenaline junkie and was fascinated by the thrill of the danger of going into the Philistine camp, getting what he wanted, then escaping. Sometimes men have a kleptomaniac mentality, stealing just because they can. Whatever his reason, Samson enjoyed the unauthorized visits to see these women. It's amazing how the human mind much prefers that which we are told we shouldn't or can't have rather than what we can.

So, the Philistine powers that be knew two very important facts that were definite about their nemesis. They knew Samson loved their women and that his strength was unexplainable. During my childhood years, I always pictured Samson as this extremely muscular and large guy, a biblical Superman if you will. I have since changed my thoughts of his physique. You see, the Bible tells us that the Philistine leaders paid Delilah to find out why Samson was so strong. **5. "Trick Samson into telling you why he is so strong…"** (**Judges 16:5 GNT**). So, in my opinion, he couldn't have had the physique of a super strong man; if he did there would be no need for the confusion. Look, I have a friend who has been into bodybuilding well over ten years. He is about six feet, four inches tall and at his largest weighed about 280 pounds. If he goes to the gym and lifts 1,000 pounds on the bench press, no one will question anything. Why? Because his size and physique imply that he is capable of lifting said weight. Now, if my seven-year-old grandson goes to the gym and lifts that exact same weight, we all would be confused. Why? Because he doesn't look like he should be able to lift that kind of weight. So, the Philistines couldn't understand how this normal-looking man was so strong, but how strong was Samson? Samson was so strong that the Bible says he lifted the city gates, posts and all, and carried them on his shoulders uphill to Hebron. **3. Then he got up, took hold of the doors of the town gate, including the two posts, and lifted them up, bar and all. He put them on his shoulders and carried them all the way to the top of the hill across from Hebron. (Judges 16:3).** During my research I found out that the city gates of Gaza weighed about four tons. For those that don't know, four tons is 8,000 pounds. That is the equivalent of him putting a Ford F-350 truck on his shoulder, and don't forget he carried it for thirty-seven miles uphill to Hebron. Thirty-seven miles is about how far Hebron was from Gaza. Just walking thirty-seven miles is incredible but walking thirty-seven miles uphill carrying a truck is crazy. That's just an example of how strong Samson was, which only makes the woman that brought him down look that much more powerful.

One of my favorites, if not my favorite, movie scenes of all time is from the movie *300*. In the opening scene, the Persian messenger has come to the Spartan King Leonidas with demands. These demands enrage the king. King Leonidas draws his sword out and points it at the Persian messenger. Leonidas stops for a moment to think of what he is about to do, for he knows his actions have consequences. In his momentary thought, he looks at his queen, and in that moment the Persian messenger's fate is not sealed by the rage of the king or the disrespectful way by which he approached him. The fate of the Persian messenger was sealed by the nodding of the head of the queen. The power of the queen gave Leonidas the strength he needed to do what he might not have done without her. In that moment the power of a woman is so vividly displayed. Her nod displayed more power than all the soldiers throughout the entire movie. Unfortunately, many women never truly recognize the true potential of their power. But the story of Delilah, as well as the character in this movie, gives a brief demonstration of the power that is within a woman.

Chapter 3

The Party Crashers

Normally when we think of an invitation, it's usually from a position of us wanting someone or something to be in our presence. We send out invitations to our birthday gatherings because we would like that person to share in the celebration of our induction into the next level of life. We send out invitations to our marriage ceremony because we wish that person to join in on the joy of starting our lives together. We even send invitations to our divorce party because we are excited about our brand-new freedom. In my opinion, an invitation is nothing more than the informing to someone of an experience life has presented to us. Now, those are invitations that are sent out to the ones that we want to join in on our festivities, but what of those we didn't send an invitation to? Somehow it never seems to fail that no matter how careful we are about our invitations, there always seems to be someone that was not invited who manages to slip in through the cracks. These uninvited guests are commonly referred to as party crashers. Party crashers show up because they saw or heard of our celebration. They stand and eagerly wait for that opportunity to sneak in through the back door. Many times, they come with less than admirable intentions. Often, they come only to disrupt and sometimes even to dismantle what was intended to be enjoyable.

Well, this is kind of what happens when God places an anointing on our lives. That anointing should be cause for celebration. An anointing is a gift the Almighty gave specifically to you. That's more than enough reason for celebration. An anointing says that out of billions and billions of people, God was able to find your location to give you something he designed just for you. He has a designated time, purpose, and reason for this anointing that will bring him glory. The problem we encounter is that once the anointing is known to be on us, and once the party crashers see or hear of this anointing, they come running. After David's anointing was known, the party crashers were throwing spears at him. **11. "I'll pin him to the wall," Saul said to himself, and he threw the spear at him twice; but David dodged each time (1 Samuel 18:11 GNT).** After Daniel's anointing was known, the party crashers threw him into the lion's den. **16. So the king gave orders for Daniel to be taken and thrown into the pit filled with lions (Daniel 6:16 GNT).** After Jesus's anointing was known, the party crashers started killing babies. **16. Herod was furious when he realized that the wise men had outwitted him. He sent soldiers to kill all the boys in and around Bethlehem who were two years old and under, based on the wise men's report of the star's first appearance (Matthew 2:16 NLT).** The party crashers come because of a destructive attraction to our anointing, but they still need someone to unlock the door. This is where Delilah comes in, for though we unwisely let her in as an invited guest, she unlocks the door for the party crashers. She is somewhat of a Trojan horse. She is the link between our destiny and our destruction. This is what so often happens with those of us who have made the decision to lay in her lap. Believe it or not, my theory is that Delilah probably liked Samson, but she liked the money more. There is nothing that suggests she wasn't originally feeling him. Realistically, what woman wouldn't? The man she was dating having that kind of power. It had to be a turn on. I mean, Samson was the ultimate Israelite bad boy who defied the Philistine authority. He unapologetically did what he wanted, and no man had the ability to stop him. Samson was the talk of the town, the whisper in the shadows, the name that brought fear to the Philistine men. Therefore, in my mind I have no doubt that Delilah originally wanted Samson as much as he wanted her. For her it may have been just physical, because the Bible says Samson loved her, but it never says she loved him. So, Delilah was an invited guest who opened the door for the party crashers. Unfortunately for Samson, the party crashers came with razor blades and eye pokers.

Though in our lives we all will face trials and tribulations that bring hardship and test, we should take some solace from the very fact that we have these trials. Of course, in the middle of the struggle, it's hard to see, but our trials are many times the introduction to our blessing. As peculiar as it may sound, this is really the time we should be the most joyous. **2. When troubles of any kind come your way, consider it an opportunity for great joy (James 1:2 NLT).** In fact, many of our blessings can't even be received until we finish the trial. You see, many times our trials are also indications that we are or have the potential of being a threat to the enemy's camp. The trial is usually the devil's way of saying, "Keep an eye on this one." In essence, this is a compliment from Satan himself. A compliment that says you are possibly so dangerous to my plans that I must put some of my best on you. In the NBA, Michael Jordan is considered to be the G.O.A.T. (greatest of all time). When he was in his prime, he was literally unstoppable. During this time, the opposing team could not afford to have only one man guard him. They would often have to double and sometimes triple team him when he had the ball. It wasn't that there was a guarantee he would make the shot each time the ball was in his hands. It's just that he posed such a threat that they couldn't take the chance. Similar to him, sometimes our trials and tribulations come because the enemy just can't take the chance. Anointing and trial tend to go hand in hand. For lack of a better term, they kind of complement each other. It's almost like God allows our trials to put heat and pressure on us to form a spiritual diamond. Much like the pressure is needed for the diamond, so are the trials needed for the anointing.

Chapter 4

The Necessity of Delilah

26. Jesus answered, He it is, to whom I shall give a sop, when I have dipped it. And when he had dipped the sop, he gave it to Judas Iscariot, the son of Simon. 27. And after the sop Satan entered into him. Then said Jesus unto him, That thou doest, do quickly (John 13:26 KJV).

This biblical illustration was used to offer or possibly explain from my personal experience and knowledge how sometimes even our enemies play an important role in our progress. As diabolical as Delilah is, she still moved Samson to a position that he was able to kill well over three thousand Philistines at one time. There are people that come into our circle, not necessarily sent by God but allowed by him to do a specific job for a specific reason. God doesn't do evil but there are times he must allow evil to accomplish the mission. Jesus chose Judas to be a disciple, not because he didn't know what Judas would do but because he did. One reason Jesus chose Judas is because Judas had something inside of him that would allow him to betray Jesus for a fee. God didn't make Judas do what he did, he just knew that Judas would. He was needed for Jesus to complete his mission, which was to die for our sins. Jesus needed someone who would do the specific job of betrayal. What might appear to be completely backward is that Jesus would rebuke Peter for wanting to defend him. **23. But Jesus turned and said to Peter, "Get behind Me, Satan! You are a stumbling block to Me; for you are not setting your mind on things of God, but on things of man" (Matthew 16:23).** Then strangely enough, Judas would be called friend after betraying Jesus. **50. Jesus said to Judas, "Friend, do what you came for." Then they came and seized Jesus and arrested Him" (Matthew 26:50).** My interpretation is that Peter, though he probably thought he was doing the right thing and had the best intentions, would have been interfering with the mission of Jesus, whose sole purpose of coming was to die for our sins, and Judas, as deployable as his betrayal was, it was progressive to the sacrifice. So, one of Judas's main jobs was to betray Christ. Now, that begs the question, could Judas have been forgiven for his betrayal? I have no doubt in my mind that Judas would have been forgiven even for his betrayal of the Son of God. See, Judas accomplished his task. In other words, he did his job and in a crazy kind of way we must be thankful that he did. His actions ensured that everything that was designed to happen did happen, so that everything that needed to happen would be able to happen as it was needed to happen. Try saying that five times fast. There are times when God must take the leash off the enemy to fulfill his plan. The other disciples of Jesus didn't have what it took to betray him. They had what it took to deny, run, and hide, but not betray. There are some people we encounter who would never stab us in the back, but they wouldn't risk their own safety for us either. Then there are people we encounter who will happily stab us in the back because they have it in them to do so. Judas was the only one in the crew who could do this job. This is one of the reasons he was hired. Much like a company that brings you on as an employee to do a specific job. You may want the job and the benefits of the CEO but may only possess the skills and the ability of an entry-level employee. Therefore, they hire you for what they believe you are qualified to do. Like Judas you are hired based on what your capability is and what is needed for the progression of the job. For this reason, God will at times allow someone in our lives who will do things that we consider to be treacherous, but even in that he still has a plan. **28. And we know that all things work together for good to them that love God, to them who are called according to his purpose (Romans 8:28 KJV).** Sometimes we must have that type of person for us to move to where God wants and needs us to be. Everyone has a job to do. Some of us need a little more of a push than others, whether that push is needed because we don't want to move or whether it's because we are too lazy to move. Whichever it is, we sometimes need an extra push. So, God sometimes allows someone who will commit the most perfidious of acts to move us forward. Then there are times God will allow evil because we won't heed any of his warnings, and we are just determined to do things our own way. These are the times that God may have to just pull back and let Satan have his way with us. Just like a good parent, though, he allows certain things even though it might hurt him to do so. But he still watches us closely with love. Do you remember the movie *Ray*? Jamie Foxx plays the character of adult Ray Charles, and C. J. Sanders plays young Ray. There is an extremely emotional scene in the movie where young Ray runs in the house and falls to the floor. This is after he has lost his sight. Anyway, little Ray trips and falls to the floor and he begins to cry and call for his mother. His mother is there the entire time, and she wants to help him because this is her baby, and she loves him. She never lets Ray out of her sight and even though he is crying and calling for her help, she must allow his pain because in his pain he begins to grow. She was silently teaching him a lesson in life. She even begins to cry herself, but she knows she must let him go through this. God does the same with us. He watches and no matter how much it hurts him; he knows must allow certain things for us to grow.

The spirit of Delilah, in a manner of speaking, is hired to do a job, once again not sent by God but allowed by him. Sometimes I think we may forget or possibly not even know but everything that happens in life is either done by God or allowed by him. Everything must be approved by God before it can happen. I often tell my kids that the approval has to have God's signature before it can proceed. Yet, every approval has a purpose and a reason. There will never be nor has there ever been a time that God doesn't know what is about to happen. There is never a time that one of the angels goes before God and says, "Master, did you know?" Even Satan himself must go through an approval process before he is even allowed to bother us. Satan, who would destroy us all from the face of the earth if he could, has to answer to our Heavenly Father. Can you imagine that? Even the devil must schedule an appointment with God to request permission to disturb our lives. The crazy part is that whatever response God gives Satan is what Satan must abide by. There is no such thing as a vote or a veto with God. What he says is what goes, nothing more and nothing less. **2. Again there was a day when the sons of God came to present themselves before the LORD, and Satan came also among them to present himself before the LORD (Job 2:1 KJV).** God even uses Satan in his plan. Therefore, if Delilah is the only thing that will make Samson turn back to God, then this is what God must allow. Remember, God didn't force anything on Samson. Samson did what he wanted to do, even with the anointing of God on his life. God's anointing doesn't override free will. Nor does God take away the anointing he gave because you misuse it. **29. For the gifts and calling of God are without repentance (Romans 11:29 KJV).** *Disclaimer: That is not to suggest you just intentionally do that.* I'm merely making the point that God knew what you would do with what he gave you before he gave it. So, by virtue of the fact that he makes no mistakes, it's clear that he knew who was getting the anointing he gave before he even gave it. Now, I do realize that goes against some opinions that say, "If you don't use it, you will lose it." And I don't want to create a place for debate, so I'll just say that I disagree. God didn't stop Samson from going his own way and doing his own thing until trouble came, much like some of us, and I'm a living witness. We want to go against the will of God until we need him to send out a Heavenly search and rescue team to save us. Like an out-of-control teenager who thinks they can handle life on the street, until life on the street handles them. Suddenly, the rules their parents were trying to enforce for their own good don't look so bad in comparison. Most want the pleasure but can't stand the pain. In many cases, we won't respond to anything except pain. Think about that little hardheaded child who you have told repeatedly not to touch the stove because it will burn him. Often that child will pay you no attention and wait until your back is turned to reach up and touch that glowing light that has fascinated his eye. The child's curiosity gets the best of him, but through the pain of the burn he learns. Now, that doesn't mean he's not going to do something else stupid, but at the very least he did learn something from that stove. We sometimes act the exact same way and will completely mute God and ignore every warning he sends. Sometimes, just like the prodigal son, we must find ourselves in the pigpen arguing with the hogs about their dinner before we will remember that "in my father's house…"

My experience with the spirit of Delilah is what turned me back to God. Not that I had completely turned away from him, but I was slowly and steadily creeping further and further outside of his will for me. This is the cunningness of Satan. He knew that trying to snatch me away forcibly would probably cause me to resist, but slow and steady would get the job done. Much like Eve in the garden, the serpent didn't say, "Here, girl, you better eat this." No, he subtly said, **"Did God really say you must not eat…"** (Genesis 3:1). The serpent merely planted a seed of doubt that caused Eve to second guess the rule she had been given by her husband from God. So, for me, Delilah cutting my hair and me losing my strength was the jolt I needed to bring me out of my daze. I remember some years ago, it took the actions of my youngest son to jolt me back out of a paralyzing daze I had fallen into. I have two main fears—a fear of heights and a fear of snakes—and until that day I didn't even realize just how afraid of snakes I was. My youngest son, who was about seven at the time, was standing at the storm door with me looking out into the front yard. Through my peripheral vision, I saw something moving. I turned to see a long black snake sliding across my porch. I became paralyzed with fear. I was still in the house and the storm door was closed, but the sight of that snake froze me for the moment. My son, knowing this fear I have of snakes, instantly went into his little defense mode. He excitedly said, "Daddy, I'm ain't gon' let that snake get you, not my daddy!" He then tried to go out the door to get the snake. My concern for his safety is what jolted and yanked me from my fear to his protection. Protecting him and keeping him safe superseded my personal fears. At that moment I was in more fear of him being hurt than of my fear of the snake. Sometimes we must have those types of jolts to bring us back where we need to be. So, Delilah was my jolt. She reminded me how much I needed God. She reminded me that I am called and anointed by him for his purpose. Her extreme is what helped to pull me away from him, but it was that exact same type of extreme that turned me back. Like Judas, Delilah did what no one else would do. This wasn't an immediate process but a slow and deliberate one.

Much like the worm on the hook, the danger is disguised as an appealing and alluring desire of what the fish wants. We can only be tempted by our own desires, so if we are tempted it's only because it's something we want. The enemy knows this all too well. Not because he can read our minds, contrary to some opinions. Satan is not all knowing. He is not God nor is he God's equal. What he is, though, is a created being that is very well studied. Let me better explain what I mean. I have three children, and during their younger years I was around them enough to just about know what they would do before they did it. During those years, if I put a Spiderman action figure, a WWE wrestling figure, and a doll baby in three separate corners of an empty room, I could tell you which child would take which toy. Not because I was all knowing or because I could read their minds, but because I was well studied when it came to my children. My point is this: Satan has had years to study our ways, habits, and desires. You see, Satan would never send a naked man to run across my path and expect to tempt me, because there is nothing about a naked man that would attract me. On the other hand, if he did the same thing with a naked woman, he knows that even if I don't take the bait, she at the very least caught my eye. It wasn't because he read my mind, he just knew from his study of me which would have the greater chance of me submitting to the temptation. See, it's not temptation if you don't, at the very least, want it. Now allow me to clarify something. There is nothing wrong with being tempted. The temptation is to grab our attention. It's the worm on the hook, it's merely the test. The pass or fail is whether you bite the worm-covered hook. Temptation is not the problem—the surrender to the temptation is where the trouble begins. The Bible says that Jesus was tempted. What did the enemy start with? Food. Why? Because Jesus hadn't eaten in forty days. What better way to tempt a hungry man than with food? You don't have to be able to read minds to know that after not eating any food for forty days, you'll get more reaction from a Happy Meal than from free lap dances at the strip club. If you notice, when the enemy was in the Garden of Eden, he went to Eve and let Eve convince Adam. The enemy didn't attempt to trick Adam because he knew his chances were less than positive with Adam. It wasn't because he just knew he could trick Eve; he just knew he had a better shot with her than with Adam. Remember, God spoke directly to Adam, not to Eve. So logically, who would be the easier to fool— hand in hand the one who got direct orders from God or the one who got the secondhand orders?

Now, even though Delilah had a job to do, betrayal is still betrayal in the human eye. It is usually one of the worst offenses that can be imposed upon another. When you have dropped your guard, lowered all your defenses, and sent home the entire protection detail of your heart, all because someone was able to penetrate your shield and convince you that they were worthy of your trust and then you find out they aren't worthy. The great activist Malcolm X once said, "To me, the thing that is worse than death is betrayal. You see, I could conceive death, but I could not conceive betrayal." Even within the federal government, betrayal is regarded as one of the highest crimes. In federal law, betrayal is sometimes called treason, found in Article III, Section 3, of the United States Constitution and can be punishable by death. Legally it is a very serious crime with very serious penalties. Emotionally, nothing in many cases even compares to betrayal and what you normally feel the punishment should be for it. Many of us agree with the legal ramification that betrayal should be greeted by death—a long, slow, and painful death. Oddly enough, most of us who agree with that thought or subscribe to that theory are usually speaking from a viewpoint of the shock of being betrayed by the ones we were sure would never do this to us. Once we come to grips with the reality of being betrayed, our next natural reaction is the desire to "put dem paws on 'em." For those that don't know, that's a reference from "Love and Hip Hop" cast member Lil Scrappy. At that moment it is a short trip from hurt to the releasing of hell. We usually, especially in the moment, can't see how the betrayal can help catapult or slingshot us to our purpose. At that time, we only see rage and what we would like to do by way of revenge. True enough though, the only reason the betrayer is even connected to us is because we gave them a VIP invitation and a certain amount of authority over our lives. Meaning the ones that betray us are usually the ones we have given the most information about us. As I said earlier, Jesus chose Judas, just like he chose the other disciples. **2. These are the names of the twelve apostles: first, Simon (called Peter) and his brother Andrew; James and his brother John, the sons of Zebedee; 3. Philip and Bartholomew; Thomas and Matthew, the tax collector; James son of Alphaeus, and Thaddaeus; 4. Simon the Patriot, and Judas Iscariot, who betrayed Jesus (Matt. 10:2–4 GNT).** Not only did he intentionally choose his betrayer, but the exact same authority he gave the other eleven disciples, he gave Judas. **1. Jesus called his twelve disciples together and gave them** authority to drive out evil spirits and to heal every disease and every sickness (Matt. 10:1 GNT).

Chapter 5

The Desired Effect

One of the most telling weaknesses within this human life is our unwillingness to control our desires. The very fall of man that disconnected us from God was our reluctance to just say no. Eve could have easily saved all of us from the struggles we face day after day with a simple but life-altering "no." In my lifetime I have witnessed the child birthing process, and I must take my hat off to the women that endure that kind of pain. My daughter recently went through thirty-two hours of labor to deliver my newest grandson. Thirty-two hours is an incredible amount of time for child birthing pain when God intended it to be painless. Wow, thirty-two hours. That's a four-day work week, and she went through this in a matter of two days. It always messes with my head to think that this pain was part of the punishment that God gave to Eve, which trickled down to all womenkind giving birth. For him to issue pain in childbirth as a punishment literally means his intention was for birth to be painless. Then I think of Adam and how he could have preserved our intended way of life in paradise by merely repudiating his desire to please and approbate with what he knew was wrong. We were intended to be born and live-in paradise. What must paradise really have looked like? I mean, a God designed and constructed paradise. We spend large sums of money for just a few nights at these four- and five-star resorts, and we call its beauty paradise. This was made by man, who is imperfect and flawed. What must paradise have looked like to the God who made the man who was able to build what we see as paradise. We use phrases like "beauty is in the eye of the beholder," which suggests that we all see beauty through our own personal view. Think of what paradise must look like to a God who knows all of our viewpoints. How beautiful was paradise for God to say, "It is good?" When life gets rough sometimes, I comically tell my wife, "When we get to Heaven, as soon as Jesus turns his back, I'm going to punch Adam right in his face. No warnings, no threats, just the raining down of them blows. As soon as I see Adam, it's going to be a misunderstanding. All this mess started with his crazy choice." I say that in comedy, of course, but I do realize it is always easiest to point out another person's bad decisions when the outcome has been revealed. Many of us probably feel that we would have handled that fruit situation so much differently, but in my opinion, we feel that way because we have read and seen what happened after Adam and Eve invited sin into the world. We quickly point our finger, all the time forgetting that we are faced with options to say no to our fleshly desires daily, and most of us don't. So, my joke even in comedy comes from a place of judgment because often the worst results of desire end with blame, and usually it's the blame of someone else. Nevertheless, the fact remains, we are in this world the way it is because of someone else's desire. **6. And when the woman saw that the tree was good for food, and that it was pleasant to the eyes, and a tree to be desired to make one wise, she took of the fruit thereof, and did eat, and gave also unto her husband with her; and he did eat (Genesis 3:6 KJV).**

Desire within itself does not always have to be pernicious to our lives. There are good desires that produce auspicious results. A desire to succeed, a desire to live a life of integrity, a desire to raise our children in a manner in which they not only will become productive but will in turn raise their children the same. So, desire is not always nefarious, though in many times and cases it is. This is usually the weapon of choice the enemy uses against us. He often couples desire with temptation, and when that combination has been married together, the fight is on. As I said previously, we can only be tempted by our own personal desires, which is what makes it so hard to say no. It's difficult to say no to what you want when it's standing in arm's reach. The temptation is not wrong; neither is the desire. It's our decision to capitulate to the invitation that gets us in trouble. Ultimately our desires, in my opinion, do nothing more than offer an additional option. Desire is not a sequestration of our will, no matter how hard it is to say no to. We always have a choice and the free will to make that choice. We have just trained, taught, and talked ourselves into believing that we can't deny our desires and temptations. How many times have each of us said, "It was offered, and I couldn't say no"? We could have just as easily said no as we could have said yes. Trust me, I know that feeling, but the fact is that our lustful desires and temptations are nothing more than that monster in the dark. Some of us who have children may have had experiences with the monster in the dark, hiding under the bed or in the closet. Those of us who have children can give witness to how this enigmatic nonexistent creature can cause so many sleepless nights. One method of solution we use to convince our children that this monster does not exist is by showing them. We have them look under the bed with us or we open the closet door and say, "See, baby, there is nothing here." By doing this, we are trying to show our children that the monster is only a fanciful thought in their minds. Still, at times that doesn't work, and it's usually not until the child reaches a certain level of maturity that they begin to see that there was never any monster nor any reason to be afraid. The Bible says, **"Train up a child in the way he should go; and when he is old, he will not depart" (Proverbs 22:6 KJV).** I love that verse, but I noticed something about it. It says when the child is "old," but it never gives a number as to what old is. See, in my interpretation, old is not a number, it's a level of maturity. So, once we reach that level of maturity, then we will not depart. Like the child, it takes some maturity for us to be able to handle the monster of desire and temptation. It takes maturity to say no to the monster. Without that maturity, we give in to it time after time.

In many of our decisions and choices, we find solace in our ability to blame the devil. Back in the day comedian Flip Wilson used those words as part of his act: "The devil made me do it." This may have been funny at the time but had no factual basis. Neither the devil nor Delilah can be blamed for our choices and decisions. Think about it. If the devil made us do it or if he forced us to do something we didn't want to do, then how could we be blamed for our actions? If our actions were controlled by someone or something else, then wouldn't that make God unjust for punishing us for something we had no control over? Yet down through the years, we have often tried to deny responsibility of our actions by blaming the enemy. Yes, the enemy does set the trap; yes, the enemy does influence; yes, the enemy does tempt, but nothing he does forces us to do what he suggests. That is completely up to us. The enemy in this case becomes the neighborhood bully who says, "I dare you to throw a rock into that window." If we throw the rock, we completely remove the bully from his responsibility because we didn't have to throw it. In other words, we choose to do wrong; we choose to surrender to what it is that we want; we choose to walk down the wrong path, and like Samson, we choose to lay our head in Delilah's Lap. We can't blame Delilah, as much as we would like to, and trust me, I want to. You don't even know how much I want to, but I digress because that's another story. We can't blame her for laying our head in her lap. God has given us all free will to decide what we want to do. Though he has the power, ability, and even the right to make us do what he wants us to do, he allows us to choose. Though the devil can be blamed for a lot of things, our choice is not one of them. I can picture Satan on the last day saying, "Lord, they are lying about me. I didn't do all that mess they said I did."

Good parents teach their children to take responsibility for their actions. I remember when I was a child, if my brothers and I did something and got caught, my mother sometimes would give us two options. The one who did it could either own up to it and take his punishment like a man or all three of us could get the beating. In a painful yet didactic way, she was telling us to be responsible for our own action because when we aren't, many times others suffer. I believe this is what God was doing after the sin of Adam and Eve. God came into the garden and kept asking rhetorical questions. "Adam, where are you? Who told you that you were naked? Did you eat from the tree I told you not to eat from?" All of these are rhetorical questions that God already knew the answers to, but I believe he was looking for responsibility. It wasn't that God didn't know, he knew because he knows everything, sees everything, and is always everywhere, so he knew the answer to the questions he was asking. I think many times we have learned to remove that fact from our minds—the fact that God can see everything we do. Often, we put up surveillance cameras because people tend to change their minds about what they are doing or were going to do when they know they are being watched. Funny enough though, we don't change our actions even though we have the ultimate divine surveillance system monitoring our every thought and movement. Still, when it comes to our children, we as parents don't expect them to be perfect, but we do want them to be accountable. We want them to own up to what they do, yet many of us want to take the easy route by saying, "The devil made me do it." The devil is the enemy, and he is doing all he can do to bring us down. He is an evil spirit with evil intentions, but he is not our controller. If he was, we all would be doomed to hell. If that were the case, none of us would have a chance for repentance because he wouldn't allow that opportunity.

Chapter 6

The Training Process

Many years ago, during my high school days, I signed up to join the military. Not really knowing what I was doing, I signed up to go in shortly after graduation. Now, contrary to what some may think, the military is a place you are chosen to be a part of. Not everyone can get in. Some, for one reason or another, are turned down. Anyway, I graduated in June and left to join the military that August. I entered what the military refer to as Basic Training. This is where they strip you of all your old habits and ways of thinking. Basic Training is a period where the government retrains your entire mentality. You are locked within the confines of structure for a period of eight weeks. During these eight weeks, you eat, sleep, and live training. From the time you are awake until the time you sleep, you are being trained. You are isolated from the world of which you have become accustomed and integrated into the world you must now learn to become accustomed to. During this isolation, the distractions of normal life are intentionally taken from you so that you have complete concentration on what you are being taught. In Basic Training you are taught all the very basics of what it is to become a soldier. During this period of training, you go through some of the most rigorous physical and mental demands. Your mind and body are pushed to limits you probably never knew they could be pushed to. Part of the reason for this training is so that if and when you are ever placed in the position of war, you have the skills necessary to survive in your efforts to protect and defend your fellow soldiers, your country, and yourself.

God does similar in his preparing us for the mission he has chosen us for. Whether we realize it or not, he allows us to go through training to build within us the ability to fight and defend from the attack of the enemy and to accomplish his purpose. God never sends us out until we are properly trained for the job. The Bible tells us that David went through basic training during his preparation for his fight with the giant Goliath. God isolated him so much so that even when the prophet Samuel came to anoint the new king of Israel from the house of Jesse, David wasn't even thought of. Often, God must isolate us from people to prepare us for the palace. David had become a soldier before he even knew he wanted to be a soldier. David's training prepared him to fight the abnormal. Of course, while David was in the field watching the sheep, he had no idea he would one day be facing a giant, but God did. Let's face it, though, after fighting a lion and a bear, a big man is of little threat. When David was in the field, God had been training him so long that the training had become a normal part of his life. We can come to this conclusion because even after David was finally brought into his father's house to be anointed by the prophet Samuel, David returned to the field with the sheep.

Let's just investigate that for a minute, shall we? David is a teenager who is the baby of the family. He is given the most minor of jobs, tending the sheep. He is regarded so low within his family that even after God had rejected all of Jesse's other sons, David is not even mentioned until the prophet questioned David's father based off logic. **11. Then he asked him, "Do you have any more sons?" (1 Samuel 16:22 GNT)** If you take notice, Samuel didn't question God when it appeared, he had run out of boys. Why? Because Samuel knew there is no failure in God. If there was failure, it came from man. Samuel knew that if God had rejected all the other sons, then there was only one conjecture to come to. There had to be another son somewhere. We can safely conclude that Samuel wasn't familiar with this family because the question had to be asked by Samuel, "Do you have any more sons?" I know that might sound minor to the point, but I keep getting caught up in the question Samuel asked. Follow me on this. God tells Samuel to anoint one of Jesse's sons, but Jesse only brought out seven of his sons. Samuel didn't even know about the other one, but what he knew was God said to anoint one of Jesse's sons. The illusion is created by Jesse that he only has seven sons, and if Samuel didn't know any more than what Jesse had shown then he had no reason to think there were any more. Except for the fact that he knew God makes no mistakes. Therefore, if God rejected the seven sons Jesse brought out, then obviously there must be an eighth. Maybe I'm the only one tripping on that. Anyway, back to my original point. After his anointing, David didn't require that his family change his positional status. He remained a shepherd to the sheep of his father, or better yet he continued his training. David didn't look down on those that looked down on him. He didn't say, I am to become the new king, so sheep tending is now beneath me. David merely picked up his belongings and went back to his training. You see, only real soldiers realize that a promotion doesn't stop you from being a soldier. You may be called to the front of the formation to be recognized and to receive your medal of promotion, but after that promotion is pinned on your chest, you go line back up in formation. God had been training David not only how to fight but also how to lead.

During David's training, God provided a lion and a bear as practice. One of the things I have recently come to recognize is that when God sends us out to battle, he has completed the training necessary for that time and that mission. Often, we don't even know we are prepared for this mission because God is so good at what he does that our training didn't even feel like training. In the movie *The Karate Kid*, Daniel got frustrated with Mr. Miyagi because his training didn't feel like training. His teacher had integrated his training into his everyday life so smoothly that he had become an expert and never knew it. Sometimes our greatest training happens when we don't know we are being trained. The training God put David through had so far exceeded the training of the Israelite soldiers that David was the only one brave enough to fight Goliath. David was the only one prepared to take on this type of enemy. The Israelite soldiers were trained and prepared to fight normal men, but Goliath wasn't a normal man. Only someone who had been trained in the Spiritual Special Forces (SSF) could defeat such a foe. So, on the battlefield that day, only David was prepared for this kind of combat. David's training had taught him that even a rag and a rock can be a weapon of mass destruction in the skilled hands of a Spiritual Special Forces (SSF) trained soldier. After killing Goliath, David added insult to injury by cutting off the head of the giant with his own sword. This action inspired the Israelite soldiers, who just minutes prior was so riddled with fear they could barely move. One SSF soldier reversed the mentality of the entire battlefield. The Philistines, who were fearless pre-David, were now running for their very lives post-David. **52. The men of Israel and Judah stood with a shout and pursued the Philistines as far as the entrance to the valley and the gates of Ekron (1 Samuel 17:52 AMP).**

Chapter 7

By Any Other Name

Often, we want to give our decisions and choices a pass and label them mistakes. Still, no matter how hard we try to shine the light, Delilah is not a mistake. She wasn't for Samson, and she isn't for us. Delilah is a choice—a very bad choice but still a choice. Often, we are hoping to soften the consequences of Delilah by calling her a mistake, even though she was a conscious and deliberate decision. The truth in many cases is simply that we made a decision that didn't turn out as well as we expected or wanted it to, and the use of the word mistake makes it appear as if it was something unintended or accidental. Giving our decisions this type of pass and power allows us to remove the blame from our doorstep or to sweep our dirt under the rug, so to speak. Therefore, if there is no blame then there is no need for change, and if there is no need for change then we tend to repeat the same actions. A decision is a controllable action, whereas a mistake has less control. If I tripped and fell because my shoestring unknowingly came loose, that can be labeled as a mistake, and the fall is less controlled. At the same time, if I put my shoes on and am just too lazy to tie my shoestrings and I now trip and fall, that was a decision because I knew the risk of untied shoes and I took the chance anyway, so we can't label that a mistake. We can't have the luxury of misusing the word *mistake* just because our results are less than favorable.

One of the things that has captivated a large portion of the world today is the gaming systems. What used to only be possible to play inside of your local corner store, or the game room hangout within the shopping center has now become just as normal as a flat screen television hanging on your wall. Personally, I have never really gotten into the gaming systems, but I use to watch my children as they would play on their Xbox and PlayStation. There would be times I would watch as they would use cheat codes to win the game. To gain access to the cheat codes, they would be required to hit a certain button three times, turn the controller upside down, kick their left shoe off, and stand on their head. After this acrobatic act, they would get something extra to help ensure they would win the game. Then there were also times that if worse came to worst, they would just hit the reset button and restart the game. The amazing thing about this method of play, though, was the fact that they could restart the game with new knowledge. Whatever errors were made before they hit the reset button could now be corrected after hitting the reset. The reset button allowed them to fix whatever trouble they encountered by simply redoing it. In the real world, though, we don't get to hit the reset button. We can't start life over and try again. Our decisions or our "mistakes" sometimes have temporary consequences but often they're permanent. I must admit it would be nice if we could just hit restart, though. Can you imagine a world that we could just restart all our bad choices? The decision not to go to school—reset, start over, and just go to school. The decision to purchase that used car that broke down one month after you bought it—reset, start over, and go to another dealer. The decision to marry that spouse that your mother told you not to marry—reset, start over, and date a different person. If we could just restart all our bad choices and redo them with the knowledge we possess now, wow! Life would be perfect. The lottery lines would be ridiculous. If we could just change all the wrong we have done to make it right, wouldn't that be a wonderful world? Unfortunately, life doesn't afford us that type of opportunity. In life our choices and decisions matter, and though we may try to change the name from decision to mistake, in many cases it bears the same effect. In the Shakespeare play *Romeo and Juliet*, one of Juliet's most famous lines is, "A rose by any other name would smell as sweet." She makes the comparison of the rose and the fact that changing the name of the rose would not change its smell. In this scene of the play, Juliet is basically saying, "I love Romeo and the fact that his last name is an enemy to mine does not change how I feel." In other words, she was saying it doesn't matter what our name is, like the roses, it doesn't change who we are. Much like our bad decisions and trying to mask them with the word *mistake*, they still have the same damaging effect. Even after we are free of that bad decision and have been delivered from Delilah, it still does not vindicate the pain caused by her lap.

I can't stress it enough—Delilah is never a mistake; she is always a decision. We either choose her or accept being chosen by her. In many cases, we already know Delilah is a venomous snake, but we continue anyway. I know personally that the warnings are usually there, but it seems to always be something about that forbidden fruit that makes us bite. For some of us, Delilah practically comes with a flashing warning sign pinned to her shirt. *Stop! Do Not Enter! Wrong Way! Danger! Fool, run away!* Yet our minds become like a deer in headlights, frozen in stupidity. Well, that's a bad description of the deer because at least for the deer there is some logic behind his choice. You see, deer are what's called crepuscular creatures, which basically means they are more active during twilight. So, what happens is at night their pupils become fully dilated to take in as much light as possible. This helps improve their vision at night. Those same dilated pupils if hit by the brightness of headlights temporarily blinds the deer because there is suddenly too much light overwhelming their eyes. So, rather than just run off blindly, it stands there until their eyes readjust and they can see again. To me that at least tries to make an effort toward common sense. If you can't see, stand still until you can. The deer lives in a world where he is always the prey, and someone is always out to get him. Usually, a mentality like that is considered paranoia, but in the life of a deer it's reality. The deer can't afford to make bad moves because if he does, it could literally mean the difference between life and death. He relies on all his senses to get him through night after night. So, for him the last thing he saw before he went blind could be the last thing he sees if he just runs away before he can see. On the other hand, the continuation of pursuit for Delilah has a lot less reasoning. We often know what she is doing and what she plans to do. We know who is blinding us, the deer doesn't, so Delilah by any other name is just as treacherous. The warnings are always somewhere that they can be seen or at least heard, but we continue to take the risk of her lap. We allow ourselves to be frozen in our tracks from the headlights of Delilah's nefarious hunting practices, making us most vulnerable for the plan of the enemy.

Chapter 8

Basic Instinct

Instinct is defined by Dictionary.com "a natural or innate impulse, inclination, or tendency." That definition tells us instinct is something we are all naturally born with. Instinct requires no formal training or instruction. Instinct is a powerful tool God has given all of us as an assistant to our decision-making process in life. It's a drive to do something by conscious will or unconsciously. Instinct can lead, guide, and even warn us of potential dangers. I'm sure we all at some point and time in our lives can attest to doing something and later saying, "I don't even remember doing that." Instinct is a wonderful tool in our lives and can have great benefits for us. In the book of Genesis, Adam had no attraction to the monkey, the ape, or the bear. There was no instinctive connection with anything God had already created, which is the very reason God said he was alone. Yet once God created Eve, Adam was instantly and instinctively connected. Adam had never seen a woman before God pulled her from his rib, but instinctively Adam knew what to do. God didn't sit Adam down to give him the birds and the bees speech; instead, God gave Adam instinct.

In 2012, I bought my wife a dog, a cute little white Maltipoo. The dog was flown in from the breeder, and I picked her up at the airport. I presented this cute little eight-week-old puppy to my wife on Valentine's Day. My wife instantly fell in love with this puppy that literally fit in the palm of her hand. Since then, our little fur baby has lived a charmed life. My wife treats our dog as if it were a human baby. We have her groomed professionally approximately every five to six weeks, but in between that my wife still bathes the fur baby when she feels "the baby needs a bath." Our dog has clothes, shoes, and even a church coat. Every morning before the fur baby is fed, her food and water dish must be washed to make sure the baby doesn't eat or drink any harmful bacteria or germs. When I say washed, I mean with spray bleach and dish detergent. Our dog is so spoiled that she doesn't even want to go outside if it's raining. She only weighs eight pounds but if it's raining outside, she digs her little paws into the floor to fight going outside. When we finally get her outside to use the bathroom, she stays as close to the outside wall as she can. She does what she has to do and quickly runs back under the shelter. It's hilarious to watch her trying to keep from getting wet. In the mornings when the ground is wet from dew, she high steps over the grass as if she is wearing a brand-new pair of crisp white Air Force 1's. If her favorite food is not in her bowl, she will not eat until the right food is in the bowl. When she goes through this denial of food, we laugh and call it her fasting time with the Lord. There are even times that I come in from work at night and my wife has the dog on the bed. This little overprivileged animal looks at me as if I have disturbed her rest. One time I came in and told the fur baby to move out of my spot. Don't quote me on this, but I could have sworn she looked up at me and stuck her middle finger up. Our fur baby knows nothing of the hard-knock life. She doesn't know what it's like to be fenced in a cage. She has never experienced her food having dirt and bugs in it. She can't tell you what it's like to sleep on pine straw and an old blanket. I often joke with my wife and tell her that she would probably get rid of me before she gets rid of that dog. There are times I really think this dog no longer thinks of itself as a dog. Though I joke about her thinking she is human, there is still something that she has that lets us know the dog is still in her. That one thing is her instinct. Often when my wife and I are watching a movie or binge watching one of our favorite shows together, we usually order pizza, the big cookie, and a Pepsi, because pizza is not pizza without a Pepsi. Of course, we can't leave the fur baby out of these moments of intimacy together. So, we get her some of her favorite treats and put her on the bed to watch TV with us. After she gets her treats, she does the strangest thing. She will take the treat in her mouth, find a little area on the bed, and begin to dig. She digs as if dirt is really moving, as if there is a real hole being made. After a few moments of digging, she places her treat in this imaginary hole and begins to cover up her treat by pushing the imaginary dirt over her treat with her nose. I sometimes mess with her and move toward the treat as if I'm going to take it. She quickly runs back to that spot and looks at me like Nino Brown in the movie *New Jack City*, as if to say, "Sit yo' five-dollar tail down before I make change." I said all of that to say that even though she has spent a minimal amount of time outside, and she is very seldom around any other dogs, her instinct still guides her into doing things that all other dogs do. She instinctively knows to bury and hide the things she considers to be valuable. Without ever being taught, her instinct tells her she is supposed to dig even though to our eyes there is nothing there to dig. She is driven by a God-given instinct.

The problem with having instinct is the enemy knows you have it. Often, he takes advantage of our instinct and he tries to pervert it. The average male has a natural instinct toward the female. It's that inner instinct that tells us there is just something about her. Even in elementary school, though the little boy might not know why at that time, he does know he wants to have the attention of the little girl. He might do handstands, try to demonstrate how fast he can run, or lift something he is really struggling to lift, all for her attention. This little boy might sit behind the cute little girl in class and pull her hair. He might intentionally bump into her, or even throw paper at her. He doesn't know why he does it, he only knows that on the inside he wants her attention. Oddly enough, sometimes the little girl even likes this little attention-seeking boy. They like each other and don't even know why. When we as fathers hear of this type of behavior at school, we have our own instinct to protect our little princess, and we might even want to fight the little boy, lol. The boy, the girl, and the father without even thinking are all acting off instinct.

The enemy is not a creator. He is an imitator who can only try to pervert what the Creator has given. So, when it comes to our instincts, the enemy uses our own momentum against us. So yes, he convinces Delilah to present what we are attracted to because, remember, he has studied each of us. He depends on our instinct to get the party started. After instinct, if we don't quickly grab control of the situation, desire kicks in, then desire draws in lust, and these together can be trouble for Samson. Imagine this: you are a man who is captivated by women with long hair and big breasts. The enemy would not waste his time convincing a paper-thin short-haired woman to come out after you. He will on the other hand try to convince that exact type of woman you find attractive to cross your pass. He will escort your Delilah into your view. When that happens, instinctively you look, and if control is not gained, desire will take over. Have you ever tried to walk a large and muscular untrained Rottweiler? He is a beautiful and extremely powerful animal. If he is trained, or for the purpose of the example, if he is controlled, walking him can be a natural outdoor exercise enjoyed by all. On the other hand, that same creature, if he is not trained and there is no control, can essentially tell you where he wants to go and what he wants to do. He is so strong and powerful that if you can't overpower his strength, you probably would do better to just jump on his back and hang on for the ride. What I'm saying is without that control, the Rottweiler is going to take you where he wants to go, not where you should go, get it?

In the old-school church like the one I came from; they made our instinct seem like it was a terrible disease we had caught. They seemed to want to cage in what was God given to be free. I think where many of them messed up is they didn't explain and teach us exactly what was happening. Instead, they just told us it was wrong and how bad we were. Then they would take us to the altar, where we would have oil poured on our heads and be prayed over for an hour to cast out the demon. Don't get me wrong, their hearts were in the right place. They only taught what they knew. They didn't understand that a God-given instinct need only to be nurtured and guided, not chained and locked away. Our feelings as boys and girls could not be stopped or locked up. As a matter of fact, time has proven, and I am a living witness that just trying to lock these feelings away and pretend they don't exist only makes them more active. Trying to lock away these natural instincts has much the same effect as it does with the dog who has been tied to the back-yard tree all his life. His entire life is within the confines of that eight-foot chain. That tree is all he knows, until that one magical day when by some miracle that chain breaks. The dog gets free and just runs and runs with no destination. He runs up and down the street looking for absolutely nothing; he is just so happy to be away from that tree. I've seen this happen before, and it's funny to watch the owner stand there and call the dog as if he is going to come back on command. What happens is that the dog has been locked away so long that he wants to experience everything all at once. This is kind of how many of us church babies got into so much stuff. Once we were finally able to get away from the church, some of us wanted to experience everything at once. Our instinct was easily perverted because it had no control and no training, so it just ran wild. Some of us turned to drugs, some to alcohol, and some turned to Delilah. Now, as I have said, these were still choices that were made, and we were responsible no matter how long we had been chained. We just needed to be taught and trained how and when we were to use them. Most of us aren't bad people. A lot of times it's just that our instincts have been perverted.

Chapter 9

The Skilled Fisherman

A t times in our lives, at least to me, the attacks of the enemy that were meant to destroy us seemed like the workings of a skilled fisherman. See, a skilled fisherman fishes with strategy; he doesn't just throw the line in the water and hope for the best. A skilled fisherman chooses the right spot, the right time of day, and the right lure to attract the fish he plans to catch. He places great focus on the lure. The lure is a bait method to get the attention of the fish. The lure doesn't chase after the fish, it just seduces and persuades the fish to chase it, and just like many of us the more the lure runs, the more we chase it. The lure is designed to create an insouciant mentality, to make the fish think more with his eyes than with his mind. Different lures do different things. Some move, some vibrate, some flash colors, but no matter how beautiful the semblance is, the lure has but one plan and that plan is death. Now after the fisherman has skillfully used the lure to captivate the imagination of the fish, the most difficult part of his work is done. You see, the eye gate is so powerful that many times we have trapped ourselves before the enemy even starts his plan. Now the fisherman waits for the fish to bite, and because the eye gate of the fish has been mesmerized, at this time nothing else matters to the fish except getting what he wants. One of the many talents a skillful fisherman always possesses is patience. With his patience he simply waits. The fisherman sits and waits for the commitment of the prey. It then becomes a game of the perfect pace. For the fish, there is a thrill in the chase, yet the fisherman knows he can't make the chase so difficult that it makes the fish lose interest. Therefore, a slow and steady pace is the plan. Slow enough to create the illusion of gain for the fish but steady enough that there is some resistance. Is this comparison starting to sound familiar to anyone yet? Millions of us have played right into the hands of the enemy because of this strategy. He flaunts the lure of Delilah, then once our scope is locked in, he gives us the opportunity to run in a rigged race. All the while he is only waiting for us to bite. But what many of us ignore during this rigged race is that we still have a chance to change our minds and make the right decision. Most of us don't, but the chance is in the chase. This time of chase in many cases is when God warns us, and warning comes in different forms. Sometimes God will send direct messages to us, and sometimes he will allow things to happen to give us the opportunity to stop. There are even times Delilah herself will warn us of the danger we are in. **15. Then Delilah pouted, "How can you tell me, 'I love you,' when you don't share your secrets with me? You've made fun of me three times now, and you still haven't told me what makes you so strong!" (Judges 16:15 NLT).** Three times Samson lied to Delilah and three times she tried to kill him, but he put his head right back in her lap. Maya Angelou once said, "When someone shows you who they are, believe them the first time." I think men more than women choose not to follow this type of advice, mainly because in many cases we want what we want. I have often wondered how Samson could not see what was coming, until I fell myself, but that's another story. There is just something about that rigged race that makes so many of us injudicious.

After the rigged race has begun, the fisherman is now waiting for the fish to bite and to give a tug of the line. That tug on the line is an indication to the fisherman that the fish didn't take advantage of his opportunity to reappraise his position and turn away from the lure. This doesn't guarantee success for the fisherman but in many cases, he is pretty sure of the catch. That tug on the line still allows the fish a false sense of assurance that he is winning and is in control. This is exactly where the fisherman wants the fish to be. Our enemy works very similar to this. He assists us into thinking we are the ones running things just to get us to tug on that line. Much like the overfed ego, once we get to a place where we feel nothing can happen to us because we're in control of everything, we are at our weakest state. It's our weakest because all our defenses are now down. So, for the fisherman that tug on the line is when the magic begins, because the action of the fish causes the fisherman's reaction. The fisherman allows the fish the assumption of thought that, I now have what I wanted. I can now enjoy the fruits of my labor and the spoils of the war. This is when the fish attempts to swim away with such an ebullience of pride over his prize. Until that sudden snap that puts the fish into a quandary that wasn't a part of his plan. The fisherman calls this stage the setting of the hook. When the fish gets the hook in his mouth, he still has a minuscule amount of control; he is not yet completely hooked. This is when the fisherman gives a quick but very precise jerk on the line. The jerk can't be too hard because it could rip the mouth of the fish, which could mean the fish would get away. He would be injured but he still would have gotten away. Much like the work of the enemy, he can't do too much and lose us but if he does, he would rather have us injured. For the fisherman, at the same time his jerk on the line can't be too hard it also can't be too soft. If his jerk is too soft this could allow the fish to release the hook. The fisherman's jerk must be perfect to set the hook. Once the hook is set, currently the fish is impuissant to the inimical environment he is now being ushered into. He might fight to get away, and in some cases this effort will be successful, and some fish do manage to escape. Unfortunately for many fish, it is now too late. They find that their fight and struggle only bring such a fatigue that they can only acquiesce to the will of their captor. Once the hook has been set, the fisherman has the fish where he wants him to be. This is where the fisherman can now do as he pleases. The enemy operates on that same type of methodology. He will jerk on the line with precision to reel us in against our will to take advantage of our vulnerability. Samson and millions of us have found ourselves in this place of penitence. A place where we realize we have but one place to turn. We suddenly wish to exchange our asinine decisions for ones of sagacity because at this point the only thing we desire is to be extricated from the chains that now restrain us. Like Samson, the wiser of us cry out with a stentorian voice and say, "Father I have sinned, but if you just…"

It's amazing, though, how the slightest alteration of our choice or decision could have completely changed the outcome of where some of us end up. That voice we heard that said, "Just leave" could have meant the difference in the suffering we are in or have gone through. That internal instinct that warned us that Delilah is the lure the enemy is using to destroy us. Yet in my experience, God always offers us a garden to perambulate through full of trees that you can freely eat from to combat that one tree that he tells us not to eat. In other words, he always has a better option for us to choose from. We need only to choose when we have that opportunity. But hindsight is always 20/20, so often the next question is, "Was Delilah worth it?" and undoubtedly the answer is always, "No."

Chapter 10

The Breadcrumb Trail

In 1812, a German fairy tale was published by the Brothers Grimm called Hansel and Gretel. The story tells how these two children's wicked stepmother would work them hard but would barely feed them. The children finally decide to leave home because of the mistreatment they had to endure. To make sure they could find their way back home when and if they needed to, they left a breadcrumb trail that would lead them back to their father. Unbeknownst to the children as they were leaving the breadcrumb trail, little birds were coming behind them and eating the crumbs. Lost, hungry, and afraid, they came upon a gingerbread house in the woods, in which lived a witch. You see, whenever we leave the Father, for whatever the reason, we become like children lost in the woods. The breadcrumbs are anything and anyone that can lead us back to the Father. The dilemma we face is the enemy doesn't want us to make it back to the Father. Therefore, the enemy sends Delilah to eat the breadcrumb trail to try to make sure we don't make it back. For many of us, we feel a sense of hopelessness in this position, and we turn to the first place we see to offer some form of relief. Unfortunately, that relief sometimes come with a stiff price because we end up in the hands of the enemy or, to follow the reference, we end up in the gingerbread house.

I can't speak for you, obviously, but there have been so many times in my life that I have turned away from God only to get myself in a mess that only he could get me out of. The saddest part of it is that God would get me out, and I would do good for a while and then mess up again. He and I would just repeat that process over and over again. I must admit, though, that many times I was too embarrassed to turn back to him. I was ashamed to have to turn back to God because he had just gotten me out of a previous mess. The main reason I would just tuck my tail between my legs and repent is because of those old saints. Those same old saints that fought against my basic instinct were the same old saints that taught me the breadcrumbs of repentance that would lead me back to the Father. They taught me from childhood that the only way to be forgiven is to repent. So, you can stand there in your pride and not be forgiven or you can put that pride away and repent no matter how many times you messed up. Those words have stayed with me my entire life. I didn't agree with everything that came from the old church, but I'm so thankful for that old-school foundation. One of the great things about God is when he forgives, he doesn't hold on to what you have done. He doesn't hang it over your head and continue to repeat, "Remember when you…" We are the ones who hold on to those things and beat ourselves up or allow the enemy to send someone to beat us up. Biblically when the woman who was caught in adultery was brought to Jesus, the Pharisees tried to trick the savior. They repeated the law of Moses to him and asked what he thought should happen. Jesus knew the game they were trying to play, and so he went along. He didn't change nor did he try to break the rules of the game. Great God that he is, he just beat them at their own game. The law said she was to be stoned to death. They knew it, she knew it, and Jesus knew it. So, Jesus didn't say she wasn't wrong, nor did he say she shouldn't be killed. Jesus merely and calmly said, "If you haven't done any wrong then you kill her." **7. …He that is without sin among you, let him first cast a stone at her (John 8:7 KJV).** I love this story because the God we serve has no equal no matter how smart they think they are. The compassion of our Lord is incredible because he could have looked at the woman and told her how trifling she was. He could have called her a THOT or a hoe. He could have done as the Pharisees wanted and killed her. Rightfully he could have thrown the first stone because he was the only one without sin. Instead, he simply told her he didn't hold this against her and to not keep doing it. **11. Neither do I condemn thee: go, and sin no more (John 8:11 KJV).** That's the miracle of our God. He knows we are going to screw up time after time. He knows that we will continuously lay our head in Delilah's lap. He knows that right after one mess, we are going to get into another one. For this reason, he gave his blood. For this reason, he died just so we could live.

One of the things I'm most proud of in life are my children and my grandchildren. I have three adult children and six grandchildren. Well, not too long ago our family was together, and the grandchildren were doing what they do best, being children. One of my grandchildren tends to get into a little more trouble than the others. I often tell my daughter that he gets in so much trouble because the anointing is so strong on his life. See, to me the anointing inside of a child is like sugar. I have hilariously watched my grandchildren get a dose of sugar in them and just start running from one side of the house to the other. They would just run, with no destination and no purpose, but the sugar gave them energy that they didn't know what to do with. So, they would just run for no reason. I believe a powerful anointing kind of works the same way. The baby has a God-given anointing within him that his parents and the family are responsible for helping him understand. The anointing was so strong on Jesus that as a child he secretly stayed in Jerusalem after his parents had left. Now, it's an unexplainable fear that comes over a parent during the loss of a child, but can you imagine losing the Son of God? How do you lose the Messiah? I mean, what do you tell God? "Father, what had happened was, I closed my eyes to give praise and worship to you and when I opened my eyes he was just gone." What excuse do you give when the Almighty Creator has allowed you to babysit his only son? That must be a different type of fear. To add insult to injury, it was three days later before they even found him. Do you get it? THEY LOST JESUS!

46. And it came to pass, that after three days they found him in the temple, sitting in the midst of the doctors, both hearing them, and asking them questions (Luke 2:46). Anyway, back to my grandchild. This particular child is extremely curious, so on this day he was being his normal curious self. He wondered into the kitchen and evidently something under the refrigerator caught his attention. To this day, none of us knows what it could have possibly been. He sticks his arm under the refrigerator in search of this mysterious thing and gets his arm stuck. His older brother comes to us to tell us that Junior has his arm stuck under the refrigerator. Instantly everyone springs into to action. We get to the kitchen and my little helpless grandson is on the floor crying with his arm literally stuck under the refrigerator. I thought that maybe I could gently pull his arm free, until I realized that his arm was wedged in between something. As I lay on the floor trying to pry open whatever his arm was wedged in between, at that moment the *why* he was in that position didn't matter. The *what was he looking for* was of no concern. The *how did he get his arm wedged* was completely irrelevant. To me as his grandfather, the only thing that mattered was getting my grandson out of the mess he got himself into. After several tries, I was able to free his arm. Once he was free, I didn't bother getting up off the floor. The only thing I could do was grab him and just hold him in my arms. My love for him was so great that nothing else mattered except my grandson was free. Even as I'm writing this, I'm feeling a little emotional thinking of that day. God loves each of us the same way. The what, the why, and the how doesn't matter. What breadcrumb trail leads you back to him is of no concern. He doesn't care where you are, when you got there, or what you did to be in the position you are in. He doesn't want to know how you got your arm stuck under the refrigerator. The one and only thing that matters to the Father is that his babies are free.

Book Summary

I n *"Delilah's Lap"* the spirit of Delilah takes on different shapes and forms. It has the ability to represent itself as whatever is desired of its victim. Most if not all of us at some point and time have succumb to the advances of the spirit of Delilah. The problem many of us face is that this spirit knows what we want. It knows the secrets of our innermost wicked desires. The things we have tried to hide from our social society. The things we don't want our friends and our family to know. This spirit lurks within the shadows of our lust setting a trap that we sometimes don't have the ineptitude to escape. We often want to blame the spirit of Delilah for our choice and then hate the person that was being used to influence those choices all the while forgetting that the decision was always ours. Delilah doesn't have the artistry to force any of us to do anything. We usually just tend to fall for the game because it's something we want or want to do.

Due to the consequences brought on by allowing the spirit of Delilah to seduce us, many times we want to lash out at the physical person this spirit uses. Forgetting that the bible says, "we wrestle not against flesh and blood…" the person being used by the spirit of Delilah in many cases are just as much a victim as we. So, when we see this flesh person as the enemy and not a victim, it creates a space for unforgiveness. This unforgiveness only increases the victory of Delilah. This gives Delilah somewhat of a two for one special. See God requires us to forgive and there is no cap to it. We must forgive just as Jesus forgave. The bible says if we don't forgive others then God won't forgive us. Therefore, the longer we continue to see only the flesh and not the spirit behind it, the harder it will be to forgive. Then the harder it is to forgive the easier it will be to again lay our heads in Delilah's Lap.

About the Author

Terrance Baker was born is a small town in the southern part of Virginia. He was raised by his mother, Rev. Pauline Majette, his grandmother, the late Missionary Josephine F. Turner, and his aunt, Maggaline Turner. He grew up without the presence of his father but never experienced the absence of love because of these women. Terrance was wed to his beautiful wife, Nickelle Russell-Baker in February 2002. Together they have three children, a girl and two boys. The youngest of the three is Keonte' Baker. The eldest is Keonda Gay, who is married to Jaquel Gay. Keonda and Jaquel have six children De'miyon Boone, De'kaiden Boone, Isabella Gay, Jaquel Gay Jr., Jeremiah Gay, and Ja'kobi Gay. The third is Jerrod Russell who is soon to be wed to his fiancé Shamese Taylor. Together Jerrod and Shamese share three children, Zyaijah Hill, Dakota Hill, and Zariah Hill. These are the people that most inspire Terrance. Through them, as well as other things, he incorporates life's reality with God's word.

In 2021 God allowed Terrance to go through some things that took him to the edge. Not knowing at that time these experiences unlocked things he didn't know he possessed. As a result, talents and gifts were exposed that were previously hidden. Though this was one of, if not his toughest test, God brought him through.

Terrance is the creator of Masculine Romance, LLC., a business he birthed to help those men who struggle with romancing their wives. God has also blessed him to start a small ministry, for the everyday man with everyday problems called, "FMO." With his wife, God has also blessed them with a couple's ministry called, "Intentionally Married." So, 2021 has been a difficult yet rewarding year for Terrance. Yet and still the word gives encouragement that, "…all things work together for good to them that love God, to them who are the called according to his purpose." (Romans 8:28 KJV).

Dedication

I dedicate this book to my grandmother, Josephine F. Turner. This mighty woman of God was a living embodiment of how faith and love is suppose to look. My grandmother to me was the equivalent of Moses to the children of Israel. She was my direct connection to Jesus before I knew him for myself. Like the children of Israel, if I was in the wrong and needed help from above, I would turn to her because I knew that she would go to the top of the mountain to speak to the Father on my behalf. Sickness had no power over my brothers and I when grandma said, "In the name of Jesus you are healed." Grandma had such a proven track record and connection with God, that if she said the sun was not going to shine tomorrow then we would look for the moon. Grandma always spoke the word, and I truly believe that I am still reaping present blessings from her past prayers. I only regret that my grandmother isn't here to see this book come to life. God called her home some years ago, and though my heart was broken at the lost, she taught me that God makes no mistakes. There will never be another Josephine F. Turner. I just thank God that I was one of the few that were blessed to experience the one that was here.

I love you Grandma.